The Things I Meant To Say

The Things I Meant To Say

E. Barrett La Mont

authorHOUSE®

AuthorHouse™
1663 Liberty Drive
Bloomington, IN 47403
www.authorhouse.com
Phone: 1-800-839-8640

Published by AuthorHouse   03/19/2012

ISBN: 978-1-4685-6075-6 (sc)
ISBN: 978-1-4685-6074-9 (hc)
ISBN: 978-1-4685-6073-2 (e)

Library of Congress Control Number: 2012904385

Dedication

for Lynn, my first love
for Patricia, whom I loved for 37 years
and for my wife, Martha, who helped make this book a reality

and to Elizabeth Barrett Browning, a distant relative, who
inspired me to take this journey

Biography of
E. Barrett La Mont

Barrett was born in Pueblo, Colorado, grew up in California, attending UCLA, and served in the Navy during the Vietnam era.

Barrett lost his first wife to cancer. His is now married, retired and residing in Cascade Locks, Oregon in the scenic Columbia River Gorge. He enjoys painting and photography.

Barrett began writing love poems in his early 20's. He is a distant relative of Elizabeth Barrett Browning, and when introduced to her work became immediately inspired.

This book is comprised of poems Barrett has written over the past 40 years.

They are both love poems and inspirational poems which he hopes will be enjoyed by readers of all ages. Many of the love poems were dedicated to his first real love, Lynn, and others written to his late wife, Patricia to whom he was married for 37 years. Some of the poetry is lyrical and some prose.

His hope is that you will be touched by the words, perhaps warming your heart and those around you, whether remembering past or current loves, friends and family. This book is meant to awaken your passion for life and the emotions that you have deep inside, and even perhaps "the things you meant to say."

A Dream

A dream of time . . .
a dream of a place . . .
a dream of you . . . and your gentle face.

A dream of feelings . . .
a dream of caring . . .
a dream of being close . . . with all its sharing.

A dream of a lifetime for you and I . . .
a dream that didn't come true and made me cry . . .
a dream of a dream that will never be . . .
a dream lost in love, but held by me!

A Love Affair with the Sea

The lady walks down to the sea . . .
her hair streaked with gold . . .
accentuating her tanned body.

As she walks along the sand . . .
the water rushes up and gently embraces her.

The breeze caresses her body . . .
and the ocean spray kisses her lips.
She is caught in the rapture . . .
of a love affair.

A Reason

A reason . . .

A reason to Love . . .

A reason to love for all my life . . .

A reason . . .

You.

A Road Travelled

You're the road I travel,
a road that takes me home to where my soul resides.

You're the lyrical sounds of chimes . . .
chimes that extend from my heart to my soul.

You're a smile that reaches out to touch me . . .
to touch me when I'm happy and hold me when I'm sad.

Our love was born in a distant life . . .
a love that is caressed by today.

And if God chooses . . .
we'll exist far beyond . . .
Where time has no meaning.

A Special Time With You

There's a place back in the mountains . . . a place that's lost in time.
A place that's so remote that only you and I could find.

It's where the dawn comes up like thunder . . . with all its majestic
grace . . .
And then sets again at evening time . . . as gentle as a breeze on your
face.

I went there to find serenity . . . and then found my peace in you.
Your touch was as gentle as the moon's beams . . . and was as soft as
the morning dew.

You came to me in the midst of the cool night air . . . and let your hair
fall free . . .
The stars reflected in your eyes . . . there was no need to make a
sound.

We both reached out . . . and our hands met.
At that moment you softly touched my face . . . time stood still and
there was no other place.

Voyagers

We were voyagers through eternity . . . with only love as our guide.
Each moment passed so quickly . . . and our love we couldn't hide.

We lived life through each other . . . our bodies united as one.
And with every breath the seconds flew . . . until we saw the
    morning sun.

As it cast its light upon us . . . I felt life had just begun. For the night
    had given you to me . . .
And the two of us were one.

April Fool

April had never been so enchanting!

The air was fresh with warmth . . .
a warmth that seemed to melt
all life itself.

It consumed us with so much love . . .
that we must have appeared to be drowning.

Deeper and deeper I sank . . .
without noticing that you had turned
for the shore.

You were to me what April had been
to the rest of the world.
Warm, alive and ready to love.

But you and April both are gone . . .
leaving me . . .
The April Fool!

Blessed Are

Blessed are the parents . . .
they bear the seeds to our future.

Blessed are the children . . .
for they are our future.

Blessed are the elderly . . .
they are the keepers of our wisdom . . .

. . . And this knowledge
given back to our children . . .
makes them better parents.

Born Unto Thee

I was born unto thee . . .
When first our eyes met . . .
Since that moment,
Thou hast been a home.

When I reach for substance,
My hand extends unto thee . . .
When my spirit
Longs to be nurtured . . .

Thou art there,
To cradle me to thy breast.

Thou art my heaven and earth . . .
And I shall stand with thee.
Far beyond this mortal being.

Broken Hearts

Broken hearts are similar
to china dolls . . .
They can be fixed
but they never are
quite the same.

Camelot Ending

It was a night . . . unlike any other,

the month was April.

The year Camelot would come to an end.

I had gone to a festive gathering, at a cottage by the sea.

When I entered . . . all I saw was you . . .

Your beautiful smile and eyes that drew me nearer and nearer.

We had just met . . . but I had loved you all my life.

With one word you put my heart at ease.

You were my first love . . . bonded moments,

only you and I shared.

Love that could be parted only by death,

we were entering a new plain . . . a love conceived in another life

was now reborn.

Children

They sparkle when they're happy . . .
and cloud up when they're sad . . .
they make you warm with just a glance . . .
and make you melt when you are mad.
They hold the hope of the future, and
remembrance of the past,
you see yourself in them . . .
and knowledge learned through our mistakes . . .
you hope that they will grasp.
they can pull you down to the deepest depths . . .
or lift you to the skies . . .
but the purest love in this old world
is found in your children's eyes.

Clouds

Cloudless skies are also void of beautiful sunsets.

Colors

You are the colors of all my rainbows . . . that
brighten even my darkest nights.

Compassion

Showing compassion to those who have none
isn't compassionate . . .
it's divine!

Constant as the Wind

My love for her is like the wind that embraces me . . .
and then moves on.

The sounds of her laughter are as comforting
as the rustling of the leaves in the trees.

You can see it . . .
you can hear it . . .
but when you touch it . . .
it disappears.

And you're never quite sure from where it came . . .
or where it has gone.

She has the power to destroy . . .
but as with the gentle summer breeze . . .
she uses her power to calmly blow and refresh my soul.

I open my arms to her
and she engulfs my body.

For whether she is near or far . . . she is with me.
She will always be a part of my life . . . forever constant as the wind.

Critics and Friends

We are our own worst critic . . .

and we are also our own fondest admirer . . .

The trick is to become our own best friend.

Dear First Love

Oh dear first love you will never know
how grateful I am for having once crossed your path . . .
on this journey.

You gave me gifts . . . it would take
more than a lifetime
to ever begin to repay.

You showed me how to love
as tenderly as the morning kisses mother earth,
as passionately as the waves are blown to land
to hug the shore.

Eternal Love

Love, like the tide,
has highs and lows . . .

But like the ocean
it springs eternal.

Exploring My Mind

While exploring my mind for things I'd like to be . . .
what comes through most clearly is I want to be free.
Free to see the sunrise and feel the morning dew . . .
And walk along the beach at sunset when the day is through.
I want to walk along the highways and byways of my mind . . .
And discover why I'm here and what mountains I'm to climb.
I feel there is more to life than existing from day to day . . .
And not finding what you want in your work or at your play.
So many go from nine to five, but merely go through motions.
What a joy it would be to take the time to navigate distant oceans.
To chase the wind that blows the sail, to feel the sunshine daily.
To go over the hill, just out of reach, and sing the song so gaily.
All these things a man can have, if he would stop to find . . .
The greatest gift on God's green earth is only peace of mind.

Fall To Me

When all of your harbors seem empty,
and sails that once bellowed are still,
fall to me, asking no questions . . . and
we'll sing songs we both held so dear.

Feeling Clearly

Clarity may be achieved by just distancing oneself from that which is unclear.

Finding Myself

There are moments when I need to be alone . . .

Not to lose you, but to find myself.

First Love

Lost are the sweet days of younger times . . .
the innocence of youth.

Such a warm glow . . . the ember of first love.
Could only the stars or the moon shine as bright . . .
reflecting the passion of a first kiss . . .
The longing felt in a first embrace and the meaning of
loves endearing words . . . spoken for the first time.

Following a Dream's Path

As the indigo shadows of night
come stealing across my room . . .
you're the last thought on my mind.

Assured of your love I fall asleep,
only to awaken by morning's light,
and in my mind's eye, I'll awake
with your beautiful face before me.

When I have moments in which
things may not be going well,
that is when I think of you.
The way you move and look at me . . .
and I feel stronger.

Frequently, I wonder if you're thinking
of me and if so, what are your thoughts?

At Evenings Tide

I often long to hold you near
and never let you go . . .
to gently kiss your neck, your lips
and your hands so softly
that words are not necessary.

At evening's tide, when again it's time
to follow a dream's path,
once again I shall fall asleep
with your name on my lips
and your love caressing my heart.

Giving

What price do we pay for love?
Do we give little and expect the world in return?
Or is our real reward the expectation of nothing,
while giving our all?

Through the giving, our efforts are repaid tenfold.
By asking for nothing and giving your all,
your body and soul, you leave yourself naked.
In your nakedness, allow love to cleanse your body
and let your spirit be reborn.

The price you pay for love may be the moon,
but you'll have received the stars in return.

God and Me

God and I are never required to meet under a roof, or between four walls.
God never has asked me to be with a group of people that believe as one,
or have set rules to worship. He never points his finger at others that
choose to call him by a different name, for whatever we call him, he is still
everything to all people. He is the first glimpse of the sun's rays
coming up at dawn and the last beautiful shades of orange at dusk.
He is the fresh smell of the ocean, as the wind caresses our face at noon.
He can be found on top of the highest mountain or at the bottom of the
deepest sea. His hands guide and shape our lives. He is all that is gentle
and all that is mighty. The creator of all the heavens and the earth . . .
and in spite of all that, he still takes time to talk to me!

Heart Dance

I missed you when I felt the cold morning breeze
that blew off the lake, where we once camped . . .
nipping my ears and kissing my face.

I think of you as I watch the evening stars rise,
and move toward the heavens
while the sun seems to melt into the water . . .
as I melt under your gaze.

I felt my heart dance as I sat by the lake,
watching reflections of young lovers
dancing in the moonlight . . .
as we had once done.

If these things are all true
why does my heart ache when
I hear music that bonded our lives,
Once we cried for more . . .
now I just cry.

How Ironic

Sometimes when the world outside and I are turning in different
   directions and my day is as dark as night . . .
I retreat back to a younger time, a time when everything was new.
We were all budding flowers in a garden of life . . . we pulled for the
   heights.

How ironic that the same things we took for granted . . . the gifts that
   made our lives bountiful and overflowing . . . are the things we now
   spend our lives trying to recapture.

One thing, unlike our youth, we find and savor again are our friends.
They are like vintage wine. With age, the more mellow they become
and the more value we place in them.
Lift your glass . . . come feast on our friendships. Let friendship flow,
as does wine and may it always be a fine vintage.

I Love You Most of All

I've loved you in springtime . . .

I've loved you in the fall,

but any moment when your next to me,

is when I love you most of all.

I Love You

I want to say I love you . . .
to reach out and touch your hand,
but also to hold your heart . . .

To be so close,
each breath is a whisper,
and each whisper would tell
of my love for you.

To know the feeling of your tenderness,
and the joy of living to love you . . .
being grateful for each day
I can be awakened
by the words that mean so much.

I love you.

I'll Be There

When night seems its darkest and shadows cloud your dreams,
just reach out and I'll be there . . . for that's what friendship means.

If you should awaken to find all your friends have gone, just turn
    around,
I'll be there, no matter what you have done.
I'll warm you when it's chilly . . . fan you when it's hot . . . give you food
    and drink,
when money you have not.

For I am your friend . . . a friend I'll always be . . . all I ask is to remain
    your friend . . .
you mean the world to me.

If I Had Never Loved You

If I had never loved you . . . I would have never felt the agony of being
   away from your side . . .
of wanting you so deeply that my eyes bled tears of joy at the very
   thought of seeing you.

If I had never loved you . . . I would have never heard the soft words from
   your lips . . .
the words that let my heart bloom like a flower, awakening from the
   dormant winter.

If I had never loved you . . . I would never have known serenity . . .
the serenity that now fills my life with more joy than I would have ever
   dreamed of.

If I had never loved you . . .
I would never have known love . . .
and a life without your love would have been merely an existence.

I thank God for your being part of my life . . . for through your eyes I
   feel I have gazed into the eyes of God . . . and what I see will forever
   be you!

If You Question

If life is filled with questions,
let the answers be filled with love.

Invisible Tears

I look at you . . . with eyes that cannot see.
I speak to you . . . with words that you cannot hear.
I move to touch you . . . and you are just out of reach.
Forever hidden by . . . my own invisible tears.

It's Fall

It's fall and the morning mist fills the air,
the leaves that once held the sunshine of summer . . .
now hold the promise of approaching winter.

The warm breezes that melted over sun baked faces,
now seem to bite the face with increasing intensity.

With fall and its warning of winter, so comes the warmth of a fireplace
and the anticipation of the holidays.

People now enjoy being close to one another, not only for the warming
    of the body,
but for the warmth felt in the heart.

This would truly be the time of man if we could only feel
that warmth all year long . . .
not just because it's fall.

Life is the Greatest Gift

Life is the greatest gift you will ever receive

treasure it . . .

protect it . . .

respect it . . .

Never take it for granted.

It may not always turn out

the way you want it to . . .

but as long as there is life,

there is hope.

Life's Storms

You are what I run to, when I need shelter from life's storms.

Life's Doors

Life's doors open to those who reach out to them.

Expectations

I expect nothing from you...
I only ask that
you try to understand...
I need room to be myself.

Look Back

To understand where you are going . . .
you must look back to see where you have been.

Love Freely

When you come to me, give your love freely . . . not fearing pain.
Never dwell on loves end, rather enjoy it and live for the moment . . .
it may never come again! You can look back with fond memories . . .
never regretting for having loved.

Love Is

Love is the sunshine that makes life bloom.

Love Like a Rose

Love . . . like a rose may wither,
but like a rose . . .
it leaves seeds to love again!

Loved By You

A word . . . a look . . . a simple phrase . . . warms me up on the coldest
   days.

Your loving smile . . . your tender touch . . . make me happy and mean
   so much.

You give me strength to carry on, in my darkest hour, when hope is
   gone.

It's hard to find the words that say the joy you bring to my life each
   day . . .
but if one phrase at all rings true, it's that I want to love and be loved
   by you.

Loves First Words

Angel soft are words spoken in a place lost in time . . .
where loves young players once learned to speak
with sounds they alone could understand. Breathing
in all of loves four seasons . . . speaking only of thee, in
terms never before heard in loves dreams.

Oh How I Miss You

Like a breeze blowing out a candle...
so you were taken from this life.

One moment you were there...
the next you were forever gone.

The words: shock, anger, loneliness and grief
were only words before...
now they've become a stark reality.

At first I was angry...
you had no right to leave me this way.

I never had the opportunity to say good-bye...
or to say just how much you meant to me.

How I long for just one more chance to hold your hand..
to tell you just how much I still care for you..
to simply thank you for the joy that you
brought into my life.

My life will go on...
and you'll forever be a part of it.
In my darkest moments...
I'll think of you.

You'll be the candle that will bring light into my life...
and warmth into my heart.

Oh how I miss you, my dear one...
sleep well...sleep well.

Maturity

A sign of maturity is when your kids
stop asking to be dropped off a block
short of their destination . . .

And when their destination
becomes the same as yours.

Midnight Sky

Thou art the first love
of all my summer nights.

Thou has left the fragrance of jasmine
that permeates my dreams and
makes time stand still . . .
for thou art with me always . . . always.

I love thee with all the depth
of the midnight sky . . .
and I shall love thee
until the last star has grown dim
and we are no more.

Moments

What is time?
Days, months, years . . .

Indeed it is none of these . . .
time is merely moments,
simply here and then gone.

Stored in the hollows of our minds . . .
moments that we draw on,
when the shadow of night fills our day.

My Bride

I always thought I knew her . . .
At least I know I tried,
But the day I really saw her for the first time . . .
Is the day she became my bride.

She walked into the chapel . . .
And gave my heart a ride . . .
Our hearts became joined as one,
When she became my bride.

The memory of her beauty will forever touch my heart . . .
And vows spoken of eternal love . . .
Say that we shall never part.

And now life is out before us . . .
As constant as the tides,
But we can face it all . . . because she became my bride.

E. Barrett LaMont

My Fantasies

I watch her from across the room.

She doesn't know that I'm here or that I'm taking in her every movement.

She moves with her own style and grace.

My thoughts caress her . . .

my eyes softly fondle her body and I stroke her hair,

becoming enhanced by her fragrance . . .

her soft skin is warm and I long to lay my head down

between her firm breasts.

Suddenly my thoughts are broken by something completely outside my world of fantasy and I'm back to my world of reality.

In my fantasies I'm her lover, but in reality, I wish I could just be her friend!

My Garden

You could never be considered just another flower in my garden . . .
for you are my garden!

Your eyes and smile are all the colors of the rainbow . . .
radiating all that is good about love and life.

Your endearing charms bring sunshine into my life . . .
Making my garden forever green.

My Martha

When you are out of my sight,
you grow oh so dear to my heart
and are embraced in my soul.

You are the sunrise that wakes me
and the moonlight that leads me into soft light of the evening bliss.

You accompany me and caress me when all others will not.
Without you, I am neither here nor there . . .
I am just alone . . .
Without you!

Now . . . Yesterday . . . Tomorrow

Treasure what is now . . .

For yesterday is gone . . .

And tomorrow . . .

. . . may never come.

Our Bond

Let the symbol of the flower and the butterfly be our bond . . .
neither asks for anything, but in their union beauty is born.

Our Greatest Love

Our greatest love
may not be
one that is shouted
from the mountain tops . . .

But only whispered
In our hearts.

Reasons for Being

Don't ask reasons for being . . .
reasons aren't important . . .
what is important
is that you do exist . . .
and existing
is a reason in itself.

The Things I Meant To Say ✸ 59

Reflections

Look at life
as though it were a mirror . . .

Reflecting only that
which is put in front of it.

Ride with the Wind

We have ridden the wind . . . soaring with the red tailed hawk . . . reaching out to touch the clouds. Let the flight of the hawk become our bond.

When the day comes I can no longer be by your side . . . never forget we reached out to touch the clouds and were touched by one another's love.

Saying Good-Bye

How do you say good-bye to someone you love . . .
someone you know you'll never see again?

Indeed, good-bye has become the hardest word to say,
so I won't say good-bye . . .
I'll say thank you,
Thank you for taking the time to reach out
and touch my life with yours.

I will grieve for you when you're gone,
but not all my tears will be shed with pain.
For the same tears of happiness
that you brought into my life
will flow again when we're apart.

To me you are like a gentle breeze
that kisses my face.
Knowing your warmth for but a moment
and yet content that your memory
will forever comfort me.

Searching

How can I reach you?

Can it be through a passage in my mind?

Do I read a beautiful sonnet and see your face between each line?

How many moments in the day I wish you were here?

Do I try to drown my loneliness behind a giant tear?

Why must I go on searching for something I can't find?

Is there no place I can go where you can't walk the back roads of my mind?

Maybe someday I will turn around and there by chance you'll be . . .

and a tear will come to my eyes, for I had to be blind to see.

Your love was what I reached for . . . and now I know it's true . . .

the things one searches for most if life, are usually all around you.

Separated Only By Time . . .

To hold you
all I need do is look
at the evening sky
and we are one again
held together by
the same stars
that blanketed us
as we embraced . . .
held together by the same
breezes we shared
a lifetime ago.

Good night sweet love . . .
sleep well.

Shades of Gray

Life, like black and white pictures, is neither black nor white . . .
but many shades of gray.

Shadows of Time

Beloved . . . there are shadows of time,
when life has come to an ebb . . .
and all others seem to exist no more.

This is when thou art there,
with an enduring smile and with words
spoken so softly . . .
only myself and the angels can hear.

Gladly, I would give up this life for thee,
assured my last breath would be . . .
whispering thy name.

Silence

Silence often says more
than the spoken word.

Smiles

Smiles say "hello" and "good-bye" . . . lighting up our faces and putting
love in our hearts.

Street of Dreams

Walk along this street of dreams . . . that leads into my life . . .
take a stroll down that rocky road, with all its trouble and strife.

Hang on tight and watch your step . . . be sure not to stumble and
   fall . . .
you may get hurt on my street of dreams and lose your heart to
   loves call.

Many a heart has been broken, on dreams that don't come true . . .
but life without dreams would be empty . . . so dream of life's joys, as
   I do.

Summer's Nights Dream

Thou art all my summer's nights dreams . . . the beauty found in the
stars,
draws your face near to my heart . . . and I feel life's joys lull me to
sleep.

Survivors

Survivors aren't those who continue to live . . .
they are people who have found meaning in doing so!

Thanksgiving

It's the time of the year when leaves turn to gold and the holiday spirit starts to unfold. When wispy clouds streak across the sky, with their message of fall, as they glide on by.

It's a time for pumpkins, turkeys, and things we hold dear, for memories of loved ones that will always be near.

It's a time to reflect on days gone by and be thankful for that we have, as we eat more of mom's pie.

For Thanksgiving is special, but not just for treats, it's a time for good friends, neighbors, and family to meet—to share the abundance of this great land . . . with a hand extended to the family of man.

The Best Years of Our Lives

Some say the best years are those of youth,
Others will argue that middle age reigns supreme.

Seniors might say the final years bring the greatest joy.

But it is my belief
that life at best is a tenuous journey.

Any morning you can wake up,
breath the air
and enjoy God's beauty . . .
is the best.

The Color of your Eyes

What is it I see when I'm happy . . . the color of your eyes!

The Keeper of the Light

Thou art the keeper of the light that moves over the blackened seas.
The candle that chases the demons from my darkened room.

The Natural Thing I Do

I thought love and I were old friends, until I reached out to thee,
now I am a part of you and you're a part of me.

The Poet

The poet uses words as his tools, the same as the potter uses the
   furnace to harden the clay.
He structures his words so they are happy or sad,
meaningful or nonsense, but always reflecting part of himself.

He has little to hide. Anyone can read his work and know his sensitive side.
They can use his words to know exactly when he needs a comforting
hand or where the deadliest spot is to place the dagger when his back
is turned.

He can't worry how sharp or dull his tools are, for he is writing from
   the heart.
His work must reflect life exactly as he sees it.

He is a weaver of dreams, a mirror of our times, a messenger of love . . .
and with words as his tools, this craftsman will always produce poems
   to enrich our lives.

The Question

I felt I was an unanswerable question . . .
now I find the answers are within me.

The Song Is You

The music is lovely . . .
its haunting sound
captures my heart
and I feel
I could dance forever.
The words say everything.
I wanted to hear . . .

They convey a message
of joy and total happiness . . .
completely engulfing
my mind and soul.
with thoughts of love.

And when I bring the words
and music together . . .
the song is you.

The Things I Meant To Say

I meant to say some things today
To talk of cabbages and kings
To tell you about the little boy in me
And the songs I love to sing.

I should have talked about the things I love . . .
The places that I've been,
The beauty that I've seen in falling leaves . . .
And in sailing with the wind.

I meant to say a lot of things,
But I never found the time . . .
I hoped you'd see these things in me,
And read between the lines.

Now our time has come to say good-bye . . .
To speak of brighter days . . .
To tell you of all the love I felt
And of the things I meant to say.

E. Barrett LaMont

The Way Things Are

Snowflakes would fall
as identical pairs . . .
Before another could
mirror you.

All that came before
has made of me,
what I am.

And when we are one . . .
our togetherness takes on a
unique personality of its own.

Thou Art

Thou art my moon . . . my stars . . . my heaven.
Thou art my beginnings . . . my ending.
For thou art my universe.

Time and Love

Love knows no time . . .
for love stands by itself.

Either it's there, or it isn't . . .
it holds no time limits.

Whether love evolved in an afternoon
or in a lifetime . . .
is not important.

For it's the quality and intensity of love . . .

That lives on and survives forever.

The Invitation

Dearest,

You are cordially invited to participate
in the rest of my life.
The purpose of our meeting
will be to share life.

You and I have been asked
to be guest speakers.
The subjects will be varied.
There will be a large gathering
of friends and family after it is over,
which should continue for eternity.

Forever Yours,
R. S. V. P.

Together

There we sat as the campfire was blazing.
Our clothes were soiled from a day spent
enjoying nature and our need for each other.

As the night cooled down and you
cuddled up next to me
We watched a blanket of stars
completely engulf us.

I felt your cold gentle face
nestle up near my neck
And with your soft kiss
we were secure in our love for one another.

And we gently fell asleep.

Tree of Life

We all are part of the great tree of life.

Some will grow into mighty redwoods . . .
Others will remain seedlings . . .

The difference is how they are nurtured.

E. Barrett LaMont

Unconditional Love

Unconditional love is definitely on the endangered list!!

Undying Beauty

If your beauty,
which brings so much pleasure
to all of my senses,
were to fade from my arms,
like withering leaves of autumn leaves . . .
I would still adore you.

I would lay by your side . . .
my eyes would caress the loveliness that
would forever be yours.
It isn't through your beauty and youth,
that fever and faith of your
soul can be known . . .
for only time can create these qualities.

The same love spawned by your youth and beauty
will forever be there with undying devotion . . .
to hold you dear to my heart
at the moment of your last breath.

The heart that truly loves,
never forgets . . .
but loves on forever.

Warmth Of Fall

You are all the warmth of a fireplace . . .
set to the music of my childhood dreams.

We are One

I reached for you . . .
and you were there . . .

Your hand stroked my cheek . . .
and my face seemed to melt
from your warmth . . .

And we were one.

What Friends Are

Friends are our joys unmasked . . .

they are the wind that fills our sails, on our voyage through life.

They are a gift we give ourselves, the one that says "open me first".

They are our own reflections, in the waters of our lives.

They hold the key to our past, that unlocks the door to our future.

Like old clothes, we feel secure in their warmth when our world turns cold.

Let the same hand that reaches out to touch their laughter,

reach out to touch their tears.

It is not to say that friends don't cause pain, for its the friend that brings us

to the heights of joy that hurts us most deeply when they're gone.

Live every moment that you share with your friend to the fullest,

for life isn't made up of months or years . . .

But moments . . . moments here . . . moments there . . . then none.

A moment wasted can never be reclaimed, but the moments shared with your friend

may be relived forever.

What Is Love?

What is love . . . it's all the beauty of life's journey, brought together to
nourish our soul.

It's that wonderful glow we experience in our heart, when we give of loves
pleasures . . .
never asking for a reward in doing so.

It's an endearing passion for life . . . sharing all that you hold sacred.

It's a candle that remains burning . . . to light our way and brings us
back to those we love.

Without You

No night so dark...
no day so long...
as those spent
without you.

Wishes

Wishes are reasons we throw pennies into fountains . . .
dreams are why we build them.

Words Spoken from the Heart

A moment of words
spoken from the heart
is worth a lifetime of
words left unsaid.

Yesterday

As the night passes into day . . .
so do our tomorrows
become our yesterdays.

And what makes our tomorrows
worth living . . .
is knowing that we lived yesterday
to its fullest.

You Are

You are in my every dream . . . and my reward for having dreamed.

You Were The First

Many had touched my emotions,
but you were the first to caress my heart.

From the moment I first saw you . . .
until your fragrance
that had permeated my being . . .
was but a faint memory
that wanders in and out of my heart.

Your Hand

Your hand is what I reach for when I need companionship . . . or a soft word.